Building in Roblox Studio

By Josh Gregory

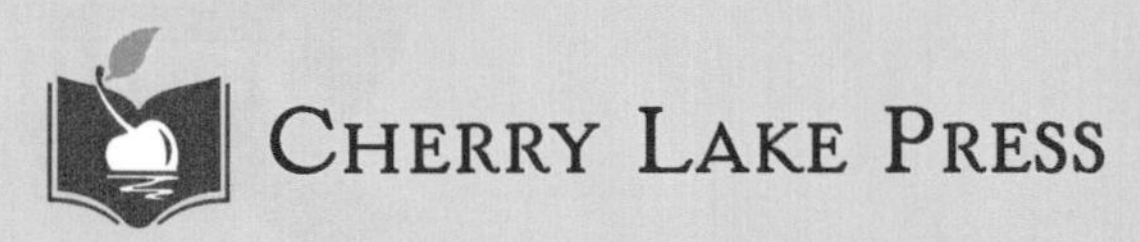

Published in the United States of America by
Cherry Lake Publishing
Ann Arbor, Michigan
www.cherrylakepublishing.com

Reading Adviser: Marla Conn MS, Ed., Literacy specialist, Read-Ability, Inc.
Photo Credits: ©Nestor Rizhniak/Shutterstock, 6

Library of Congress Cataloging-in-Publication Data has been filed and is available at catalog.loc.gov

Cherry Lake Publishing would like to acknowledge the work of the Partnership for 21st Century Learning,
a Network of Battelle for Kids. Please visit *http://www.battelleforkids.org/networks/p21* for more information.

Printed in the United States of America
Corporate Graphics

Table of Contents

Your Very Own Video Game 5
What You Need 7
Trying a Template 9
Controlling the Camera 11
The Explorer Window 13
Putting Pieces Together 15
Time for Testing 17
Share Your Creations 19
What Will You Build? 21
Glossary 22
Find Out More 23
Index 24
About the Author 24

Roblox has millions and millions of games to choose from. Some are very simple, while others are quite complex.

Your Very Own Video Game

Have you ever wanted to make your own video games? Getting started is easier than you might think. Have you ever played *Roblox*? Millions of people log on to this program every day to play games. All of the games they play are created by other players! You can be one of these creators. All it takes is a good idea and a little hard work.

Ask a parent or trusted adult to help you download and install *Roblox* Studio.

What You Need

To make *Roblox* games, you need to download a program called *Roblox* Studio. This program is completely free. You can get it by visiting *www.roblox.com/create*. It only works on Windows and Mac PCs. That means you need a laptop or desktop computer. You can't build *Roblox* games on an iPad, mobile device, or game console. At least not yet!

All Templates Theme Gameplay

Baseplate

Flat Terrain

Village

Castle

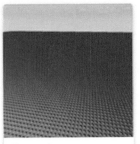

Pirate Island

Western

City

Obby

Infinite Runner

Capture The Flag

Team/FFA Arena

Combat

Would you rather start with an empty game instead of using a template? Choose “Baseplate” or “Flat Terrain.”

Trying a Template

Open *Roblox* Studio after you install it. You should see a screen where you can choose what kind of game you want to make. Try picking one of these **templates**. A good one to start with is called "Obby." This will let you design a simple obstacle course. Click on the template you like. Then the main *Roblox* Studio screen will load.

Ask for Advice

Is there something specific you want to put in your game? If you don't know how to do it, look online. There are tons of helpful **tutorial** videos on YouTube and other sites.

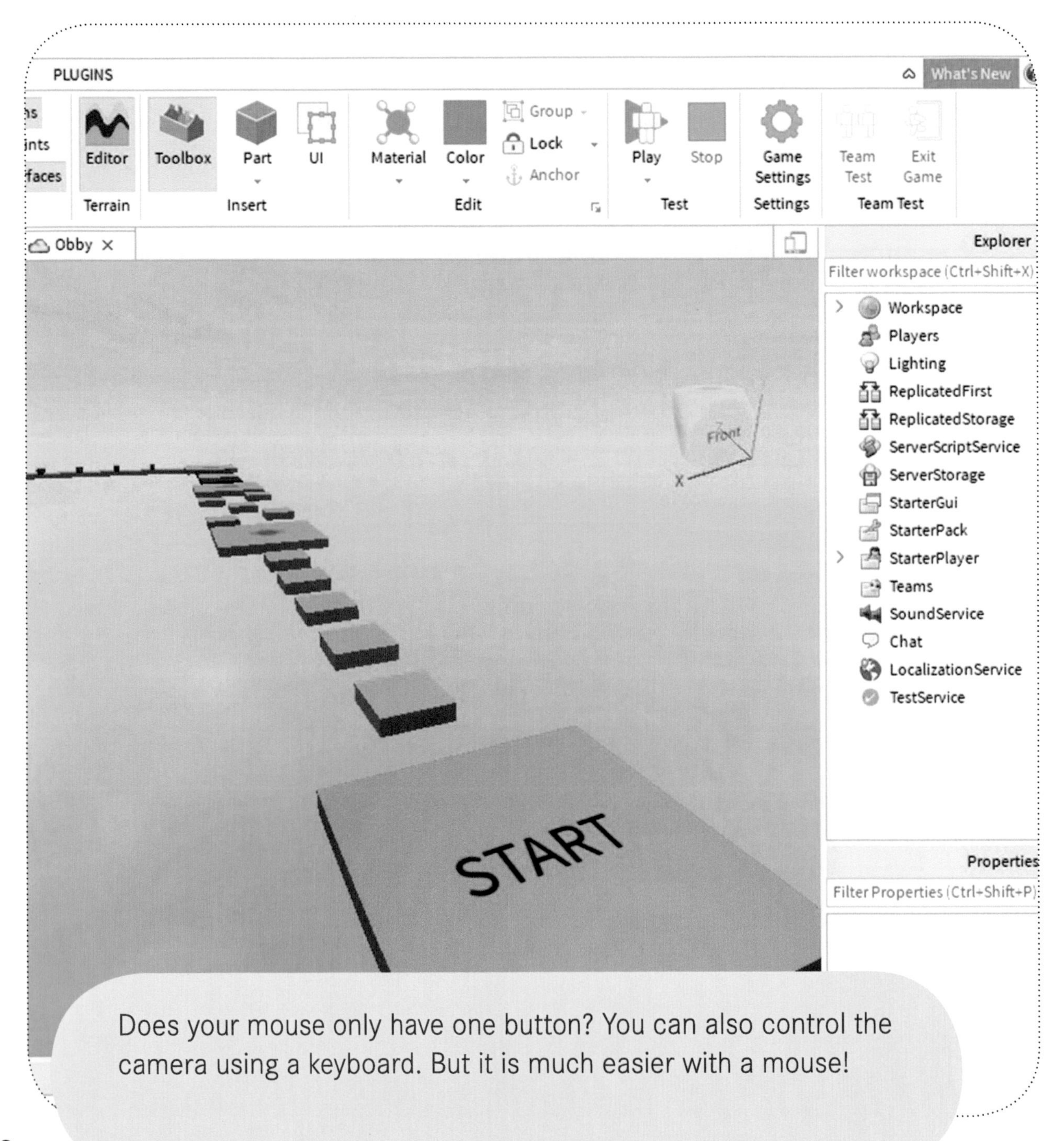

Does your mouse only have one button? You can also control the camera using a keyboard. But it is much easier with a mouse!

Controlling the Camera

You should now see something that looks like a *Roblox* game in the center of your screen. Around it are a bunch of menus and windows. Place your cursor over the center window. Hold down the right mouse button and drag your mouse. You will move the camera angle. Scroll your mouse wheel up and down to zoom. Click and hold the wheel, then drag your mouse. This moves the camera's location.

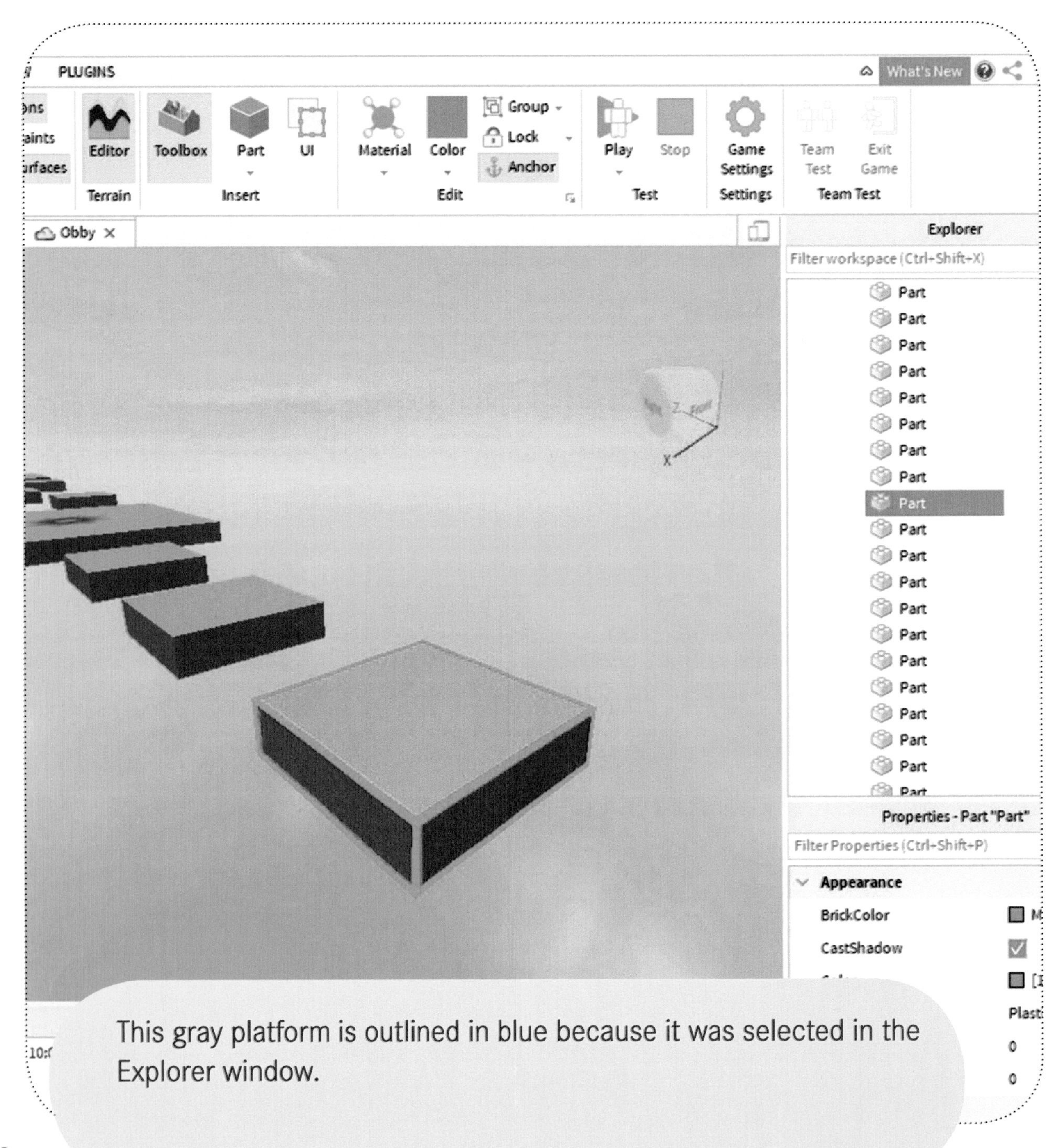

This gray platform is outlined in blue because it was selected in the Explorer window.

The Explorer Window

You should see a window titled "Explorer" on the right side of your screen. This window lists all of the objects in your game world. Click one of the items on the list. You should see a blue box pop up around that object in the center window. Or you can click on an object in the center window. It will then be highlighted in blue in the Explorer window.

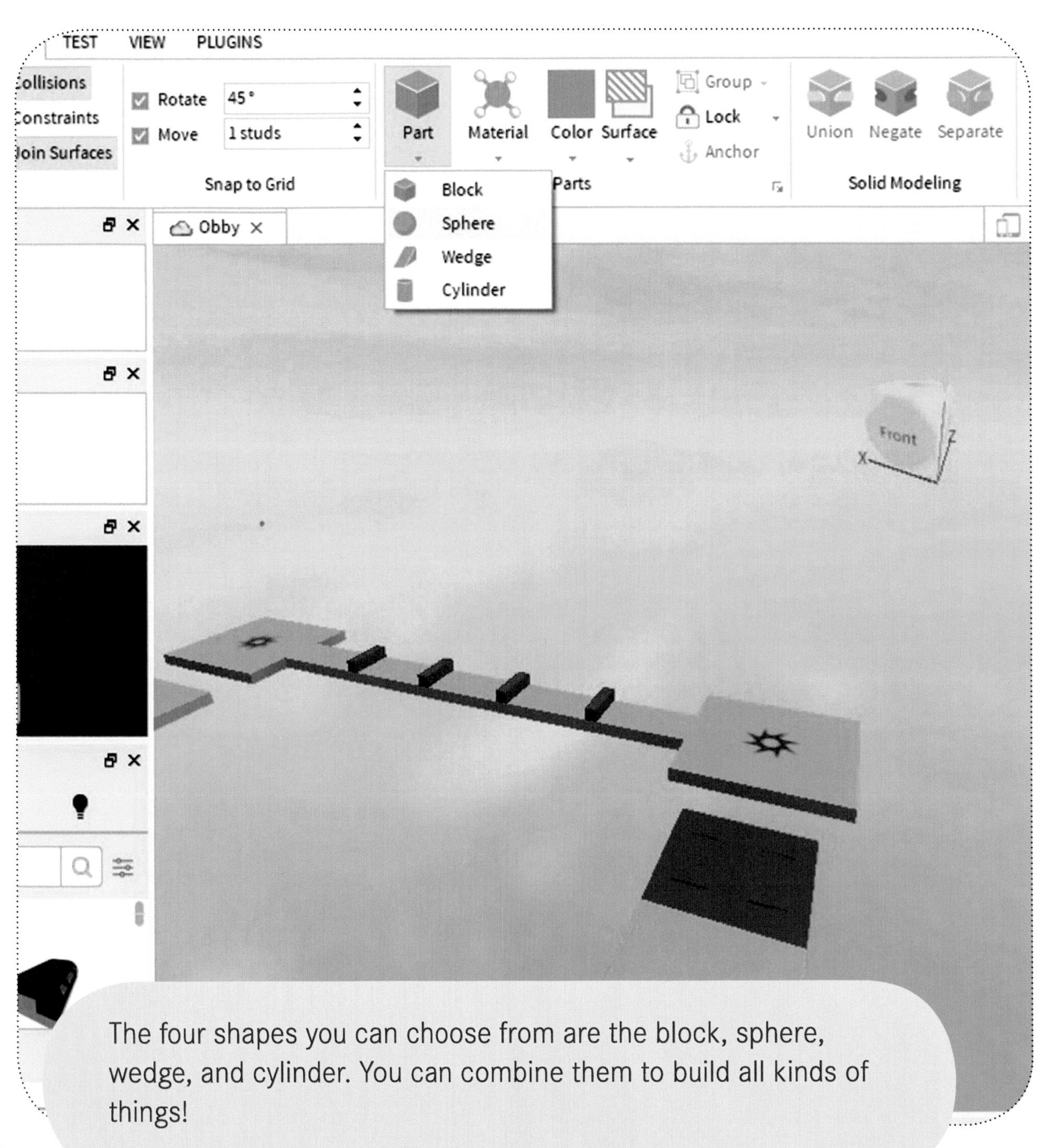

The four shapes you can choose from are the block, sphere, wedge, and cylinder. You can combine them to build all kinds of things!

Putting Pieces Together

Now it's time to add objects to your game. Near the top of the screen, click on "Model." Then choose "Part." There are four shapes to choose from. Click one. It will show up in the center window. Now you can click and drag it to move it around. Create more parts and arrange them to build bigger things.

More to Explore

On the left side of the screen is a window labeled "Toolbox." It is full of objects such as trees and cars. You can click and drag these objects right into your game world!

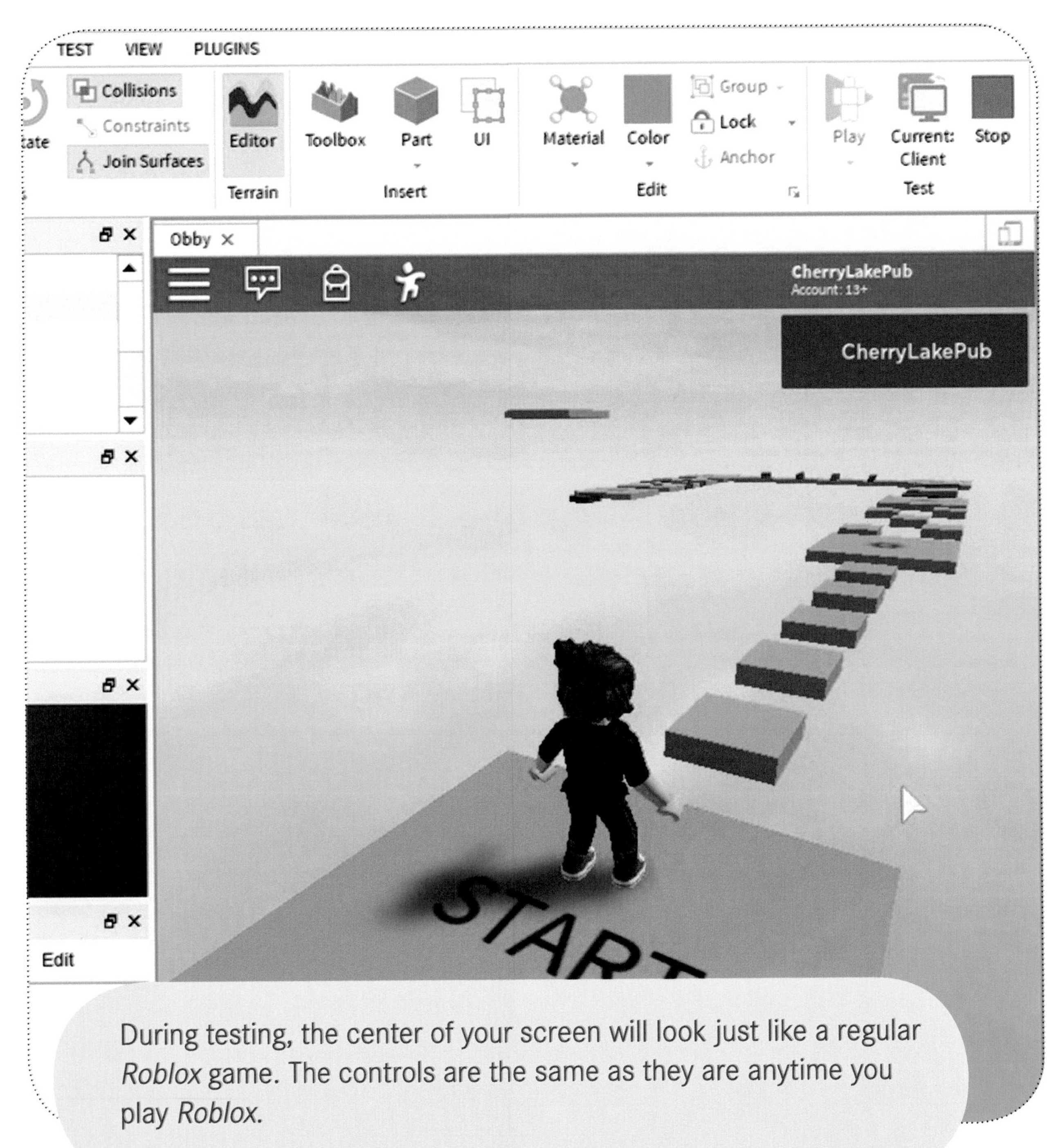

During testing, the center of your screen will look just like a regular *Roblox* game. The controls are the same as they are anytime you play *Roblox*.

Time for Testing

Are you ready to try out your game? In the top left corner of the screen there is a button that looks like a triangle with a *Roblox* character in front of it. Click this button. Your *Roblox* **avatar** will appear onscreen in your game world. You can run around and explore your creations! To go back to building, click the same button again. (It will now be a red square.)

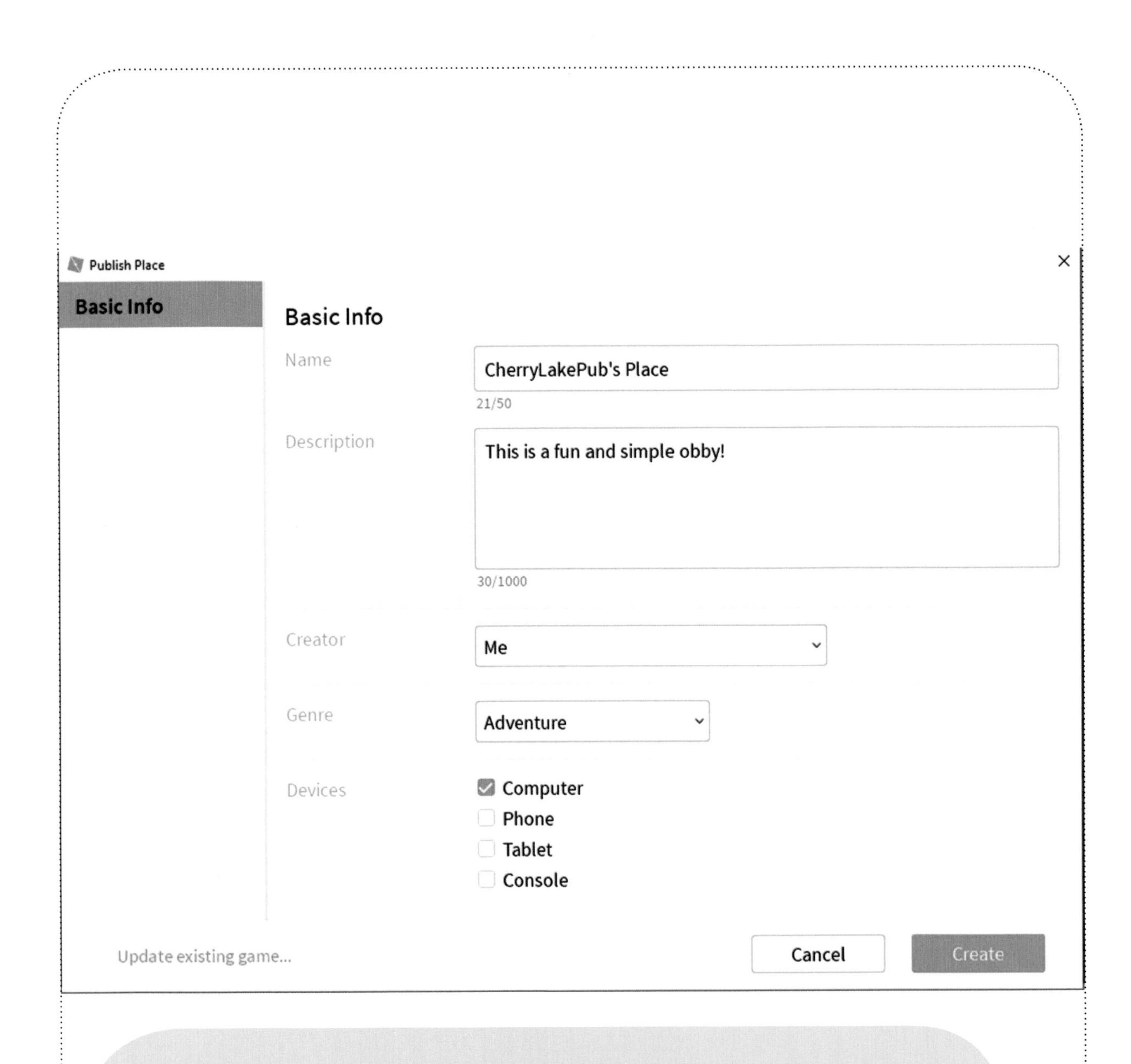

Give your game a good description that will make other players want to try it.

Share Your Creations

Are you ready to share your work online? Click "File," then "Publish to Roblox." Then click the button that says "New Place." Give your game a name and write a short description. Then choose what **genre** your game belongs to. Finally, decide which systems people can use to play your game.

Before you know it, you'll be creating amazing-looking games like this!

What Will You Build?

There is a lot more to learn about *Roblox* Studio. This program is very powerful. You can use it to create almost anything you imagine. All it takes is practice! Try to learn something new every time you work on a project. You'll be surprised how quickly you become a skilled game designer!

Keep At It!

Don't be frustrated if you don't master the details of *Roblox* Studio right away. It is a complex program. Even skilled users will take a long time to get good at it!

Glossary

avatar (AV-uh-tar) a character that represents you in a video game

genre (ZHAHN-ruh) a category of video games

templates (TEM-plits) pre-built levels you can change and build upon in *Roblox* Studio

tutorial (too-TOR-ee-uhl) a video where someone explains how to do something

Find Out More

Books

Cunningham, Kevin. *Video Game Designer*. Ann Arbor, MI: Cherry Lake Publishing, 2016.

Powell, Marie. *Asking Questions About Video Games*. Ann Arbor, MI: Cherry Lake Publishing, 2016.

Web Sites

Roblox
www.roblox.com
Sign up for a *Roblox* account, download the game, and start playing.

Roblox Support
https://en.help.roblox.com/hc/en-us
Find answers to common questions about *Roblox* and check out some guides to getting started.

Index

avatar button, 17

camera angle, 11
computers, 7

descriptions, 19
downloads, 7

exploration, 17
"Explorer" window, 13

genres, 19

"Model" option, 15

names, 19

"Obby" template, 9
objects, 13, 15

"Part" option, 15
practice, 21

shapes, 15
sharing, 19

templates, 9
"Toolbox" window, 15
tutorial videos, 9

About the Author

Josh Gregory is the author of more than 150 books for kids. He has written about everything from animals to technology to history. A graduate of the University of Missouri–Columbia, he currently lives in Chicago, Illinois.